LIGHT IN THE
DARKNESS

Julie Bergstrom

LIGHT IN THE DARKNESS:
A mother's personal journals after the death of her son

Copyright (c) 2012 by Julie Bergstrom

Createspace

Non Fiction/ Inspirational/ Recovery

ISBN-13: 978-1480293816

ISBN-10: 1480293814

This book is dedicated

in Loving Memory of my son

Jonathon Michael Bergstrom

July 5, 1987 - August 23, 2007

Thank you to all who were/are part of my healing process...
I am truly grateful. A special thank you to Life Coach,
Margee...your coaching took me from random thoughts in many,
many notebooks to a workable product that is now this book we
hold in our hands.

~ ~ ~ ~ ~

The depth of my suffering is difficult to summarize, how do I put into words how it feels? If you are reading this, I probably don't need to, you are living it.

I struggled to know how to present this book to you. What could I say to help bring a little breath back into your lungs or give you a glimmer of hope at a time when all seems lost? I think back to the days and months after my son died and after the initial numbness slightly subsided I turned to books. I had a strong urge to read about death, the afterlife and other people's experiences in both. I was searching for comfort in those books. Others had been where I am, I needed to know how they made it through...that years later it was possible to still be breathing, still living. I needed to know that I was not alone and I want you to know...NEITHER ARE YOU.

~ ~ ~ ~ ~

My purpose for this book is to show you through my words and experiences that there is still hope, there is still love. Amidst all the chaos and pain there are treasures to be grateful for. We can either allow our pain and suffering to keep us down and hold us back from life and the people that still need us or we can allow it to open our eyes to all the things that we are and can become through a new appreciation for life. My son's death has opened my eyes to the greatest gift...Hope, True Hope, something I never really understood until now.

I am always going to long for my son, I will always miss what could have been, but I am also going to enjoy every single moment I am given on this earth to share with the people I still have in my life. I still have a son that loves and needs me. I still have family and friends that care about me. I still have plenty to be thankful for. If I allow myself to wallow in self-pity for too long, I will miss many wonderful moments with these people and many new opportunities in life and I refuse to do that. The people we have lost would not want us to spend our lives grieving for them. They loved us; they would want us to find happiness.

I guess the best way to start, is to tell you who I am to be writing this book. I have no special degrees, diplomas or awards, I am simply and complicatedly someone who suffers great sorrow and who continually makes a conscious effort to rise above and grow from it.

For as long as I can remember I have wanted to write a book, and now I have written this book, one of my life's goals accomplished. Although, the thrill I expected is minimized due to the nature of the book and to the fact that the three people in my life that appreciated and encouraged my writing the most are no longer with me…my mom, my dad and my son Jonathon. They were all writers, avid readers or both and they understood my passion for words. There is much sorrow attached to this book…a mother's journey through despair, but there is also so much more…there is hope and love, strength and courage.

This book is about reaching out to others, offering a glimpse of hope during a time of great despair. This book is about my expression of grief, the moments of clarity and the strength of my God. This book is a look through my personal journals as I struggle to make sense of the tragedy that has become my life.

For a couple months after my son Jonathon died, I did not write, I could barely breathe, let alone form any kind of sentence or thought process. How I got through those days and weeks that followed, I'm not quite sure. Many people came to help us and support us. My son's friends were plentiful and such a great comfort to me, I wanted nothing more than to be near them, listening to their stories of him. I remember for months, waking up to the horrible realization that my son was gone. My creative, intelligent, witty child is no more. No words can describe that feeling.

In times of tragedy, pain and despair, a person's true self shows... I have a new found respect for a few people in my life, the people that have really been there for me, going above and beyond, helping make our pain, a little more bearable. The adequate words to thank them are not even in my vocabulary, I am truly grateful.

~ ~ ~ ~ ~

My son Jonathon was killed in a car accident when he fell asleep while driving home from work. It was the morning of August 23rd, 2007, he was 20 years old. A date and memory forever etched in my heart. A tragedy like this is not something you are ever prepared for, a bombardment on all your senses and everything you hold so dear in your life. Only two and half months have passed as I write this, needing the release of emotions and feelings that are too difficult to bear. I want my son back! I want my life back! I want to feel whole and happy and yet I know I will never have what I want. What I know is that what I have today, I may not have tomorrow. What I know is that my life will continue, must continue, one day at a time. What I know is that I still have a living son that needs me.

October 06, 2007

The pain is immense, the sorrow embedded, I have a permanent knot in my stomach and a steel rod in my back. A mother is always and never prepared for this pain. We fear this throughout our children's lives, but never and always believe it can happen. "Look both ways, don't talk to strangers, drive safe, buckle up, and be careful..." have been my constant reminders. We put our whole heart and soul into their safety and happiness. That is our purpose, to be the parent, to give and teach and love...completely, unconditionally. How then can a mother, a parent endure the utter retching heartbreak of the death of a child? I am told that we do, I think that I will, because I am still a mother, I still have a child to give, teach and love. I utter the same warnings; I still love completely and unconditionally. How? Why? Because I am still Mom, I made a promise to my children at birth, to be there, always and I will be there for my children...one living, one dead.

We grow with our children. We learn and teach each other life's lessons. As a parent we hope and pray we are making good choices for our children. What a parent feels for a child is not easily explained, it is a bonding to your heart, when your child is happy, you are happy, when your child suffers, you suffer; the connection so strong, yet so fragile.

There is part of me that is relieved that my son has no more worries, no more grief and unfairness, no more feeling like he doesn't fit in. I am confident he is at peace and experiencing a much greater sense of being. I picture him in a heavenly library with millions of books and scrolls…more information than he could ever hope to have at his fingertips. I see him quietly, peacefully playing his guitar. I imagine him in a roomful of intellectuals, discussing and debating anything and everything. I believe he was put on this earth to learn tolerance and to share his belief and ideas on living as your true self.

I miss him with all of my heart and I am truly grateful to God for the days I was given to share with him. I long to be with him again, to hold him and hear his voice, I am not afraid to join him, when my time comes…I look forward to that day.

November 07, 2007

At a loss for words

Feeling so intense

Burning deep inside

The pain is too immense

Longing for your voice

The feel of your embrace

What I wouldn't give

Just to gaze upon your face

November 10, 2007

My mom is dying...she was diagnosed with Pancreatic cancer and given 5 months to live...5 months ago. I feel her slipping away. I struggle between wanting her to comfort me in my grief and me wanting to comfort her in her dying. I know she struggles with it too. How sad and scared she must feel wanting to be there for her child and knowing that she won't be around much longer and that I will have to deal with that as well. I want to lay my head in my mom's lap and have her take away my pain...but for the most part I show her my strength, the strength that I inherited from her. I don't want her to worry too much about me; although I know she does...she's my mom.

Life is really, really hard right now and I just don't know how much more I can take...will there be a breaking point? I don't want my mom to die...I need her.

~ ~ ~ ~ ~

Is this me, this person I see?

Cold eyes, stiff spine

Standing up strong,

Pretending I'm fine

Who am I? What am I? The definition is gone;

Mother, Daughter, Worker, Wife

All these years, is this my life?

What's the next step? Do I take it alone?

I'm scared and confused,

My senses have gone

November 27, 2007

When dealing with grief, the feelings are so raw, so bare. I just don't know what to do with them. I don't know who I am or what I will become. How will I carry on and do I even want to? I'm torn between two worlds; both hold people that are so dear to me... I'm weary in one and overwhelmed by possibilities of the other. Life is life is life...the only real choice is to keep moving forward. We are born to survive, to live, to learn, to love and to experience. Life does go on, with or without me or my loved ones. Death is part of life, whether we accept it or not. I will continue on with my life, it will be a new life, a very different life...I'm more stay than go.

December 01, 2007

My grieving has made me question my current parenting skills. Yes, I am still always available to listen or give advice, but I question my advice, I feel that my thoughts and feelings and ideas are all confusing. I had spent all of my motherhood doing those things and much, much more and in the end all my precautions and worry and care couldn't have and didn't save my son. I feel the advice I give is wasted and useless. It may sound good, it may make perfect sense but, they don't always use it, sometimes your kids will make horrible decisions; they may risk their lives and sometimes the lives of others. We need to allow our kids to be who they are but also hold them accountable for their choices. We all hate to see our kids suffer, be sad, or hurt, but that is the stuff that shapes our lives. Sometimes, life can be hard; relationships can be hard; living can be hard; and the sooner we learn to work through the tough things in life the better able we are to enjoy the good things. I believe we become a more complete person because of the struggles we work through and obstacles we overcome. Life can also be very good. We need people in our lives to share our happiness and sorrow; those are the blessing in life…the wonderful relationships we build, family, friends, even pets, all help keep us fulfilled. These are the things that inspire us to get out of bed every morning; these are the things that get us through our days.

Thoughts of my children have always filled my days; what they were doing, something I wanted to talk to them about, etc... I think back to when I was younger, as a kid, a teenager and even as an adult. No matter what I was feeling, just hearing my mom's voice always comforted me. I'd like to think my kids feel the same. Now that I have lost Jonathon I find him in my thoughts more often, it's as if I feel his presence in my every breath. I miss him every minute of every day.

It comes to me in waves

GRIEF-PAIN-STRENGTH

I feel strong and able, then weak and broken.

I am a child who needs her mother

But I haven't one

I am a mother who yearns for her child

But he has died.

I am a fragile being, who doesn't have a clue

What do I do? Where do I turn?

My mind so full it hurts

My heart so broken it bleeds

December 19, 2007

Bewildering- the feeling of being torn between life and death-Joy and Sorrow...

One child has died, one child is living. Torn between my loyalties, am I grieving enough, too much, too little????? Sorrow, pain, longing and despair are my companions, Joy, Hope and Strength are fleeting. Blindly trudging along, no cares, no meaning, just life...never the same, always something missing...just beneath the surface.

If you were standing before me
I know just what I'd do
I'd lay my hands upon your face
Looking into your eyes of blue
I'd gaze upon your dimpled cheeks
The cleft left in your chin
I'd touch the smoothness of your hair
My heart would burst from within
I'd whisper that I love you
And I miss you every day
You'd smile at me and give that grin
To let me know that you're okay

New thought...

Life never looks like this when we are young. We dream of big things. We dream of love and a home, family, our careers and all the possibilities that come with those things. Never once when growing up did I think about the possibilities of my babies dying, of my life falling apart. I have been faced with the cold, hard truth...it is possible for my children to die, it is possible to be hurt beyond repair, it is possible for life to knock you flat on your ass AND, it is also possible to pick yourself up and keep going forward.

God is in me I feel his strength, his love. At moments so strong! I pull my strength and my breath from God; where else would I find it? In a family of selfishness and vanity, in a father that doesn't see me; in a mother that didn't have enough time and now has none? Where do I find hope and comfort if not with God? God, I give it all to you and ask for the courage to fulfill my purpose in your eyes.

January 04, 2008

The pain I feel must be written on paper, it cries out to be recorded. It is real and I don't know what else to do with it. Who will get me through this? Who gives me the strength each morning to open my eyes and crawl out of bed? I'm confused, scared and sad…I know I have to be strong and hold on, but today I don't want to…I want to be free from this painful, heart wrenching feeling, I want to be with Jonathon and have no more worries…

I'm not afraid to die…whatever it holds I am prepared to welcome it, sooner than later. I long to be out of this cold, hard world…

New thought...New day

I've always believed that anything could be made better...What does a person do when there is nothing to be done? What is the course of action, the game plan when the game can't be won? I have been thrown from my comfort zone into a painful reality. I don't trust my judgment, my thoughts, opinions...who am I, what am I supposed to do? My thoughts are jumbled even as I write...I DON'T WANT TO DO ANYTHING! I want to curl up in a ball, right here, right now and go to sleep...no thinking, no worrying, no feeling, no nothing. I want it all to go away; I want to be happy, I want my son back!!! Yet amidst these feelings is the knowledge that I will see him again one day, I feel his love and know that I will have that with me forever. Am I crazy? One moment I am in the depths of despair and the next grateful for all that I have been blessed with. In my sadness I seem to always search for hope, surprisingly I am not a quitter as I once would have thought of myself. This impresses yet confuses me...

January 14, 2008

What advice could I possibly offer to a fellow grieving parent? I am barely staying afloat myself, but yet I yearn to reach out to others. Maybe my writing is a way to help other parents through their grief. I think that may be the only way I will make it myself is by guiding someone else. God has and will continue provide me with the necessary tools to do this.

March 04, 2008

Today is my son Josh's 17th birthday. I realize today that one of the biggest things I wanted my kids to know was that "I have been a child, an adolescent, a teenager, a young adult...I have passed through these stages, I have had similar experiences, and I do get where you are coming from. I have learned a few lessons in those years and I actually have some knowledge that could assist you, if you could only open your mind to it."

Happy Birthday Josh...I pray you know how very dear you are to my heart.

Later, same day…

I think often of other parents I know that have lost a child…I wonder, do they think of me?

Many times Jonathon's accident has run through my head. I wasn't there but there is a strong need to be there, to know the moment my son left this life. I imagine what his last thoughts were, what was the last thing he saw, felt. I'd like to believe that as he fell asleep at the wheel, he had a pleasant dream image playing through his mind and then unconsciousness. I'd like to believe that he was dreaming then he felt peace…God.

I was with him the moment he met this world, I should have been there the moment he left. I wasn't meant to be, I guess. But I relive those moments as though I was, I have always experienced the sadness, joy and pain that he had felt in this world right along with him, from a different perspective.

March 06, 2008

I have tight knot between my shoulder blades...a heavy, weighty feeling upon my chest. Days that pound emotions through my senses...confusion, numbness and a feeling I will never be able to explain. Others know I am a member now...they'll know my heart.

The life force in me must be incredibly strong...for I feel as though I don't want to live, can't bear the pain nor take one more breath, yet, I am here, I am breathing, I am walking, talking- I am living. There is energy in me that won't let me quit...that makes me go on, that gives me hope. Hope that gives me breath, and breath that gives me courage. I am drawn to believe that by assisting others I will heal my soul for I do not know how to heal on my own. I can't see what lay ahead... unless I'm looking through someone else's eyes.

Will I forget...the sound of your voice, the look in your eyes, the feel of your embrace, the joy of your laughter? Will I forget the conversations we've had, the tears that we cried, and the love that we felt? Will I always know the wisdom you left me, the courage life takes? Only time will tell, all I can do is hope; tomorrow will be what it I make it. I feel I am in a better place to handle my heartache because of past life events. I've been through a year's worth of amazing seminars on self-awareness, and taking responsibility for our lives. I've also learned the difference between "responding" to life instead of "reacting." It has definitely been a benefit to me, and it has given me a strong desire to share my knowledge with others and to truly make a difference in someone else's life. I believe we are all special in one way or another, we all have something of benefit to offer the world, and it is a matter of choosing to do so or not.

March 08, 2008

I feel numb today...I have no emotions. I am going through the motions of life. I am heading to the bottom, with no way to stop it in sight. No one can help me. No feeling, no thought. I have thought myself out...so many things going through my head, my brain just said, "Stop!, Enough!" I need a break. Just use the basic functions...see, hear, breathe, and move. Okay.

Memories and emotions scrambling around in my head;
What is real? What is important?
Minutes and hours of dread
Nothingness threatens to swallow me
In my heart I want to give in
Pushing and dragging through my days
Dreading when a new one begins

March 09, 2008

I write this book randomly, for that is how my thoughts come. I want to put into words what I am feeling and the revelations that I am having in hopes that some other parent will be comforted in some way by my words as I am comforted by others. If in my pain and grief I can do some good then that is part of my purpose. For I believe that we do have a purpose and everything that happens can teach us something new. Giving us perspectives we didn't have before, opening doors, expanding our lives. We will suffer and have pain, but we will also have joy, and love and that is what makes it all worthwhile. The happiness that we experience has to somehow make up for the other. It's up to us to find a way to make that happen. We are only wasting our time here if we don't learn from our experiences and use them to shape our lives in a more purposeful way. If you lose a child, the least you learn is how fleeting life can be. The least you can learn is to appreciate the life around you and those you love. I've learned that I have more strength in me than I ever, ever imagined possible. I've learned that I am a good parent

…as I look back on my child's life; I have found very few regrets, words left unspoken, moments passed by. I believe I gave my son all that I had to offer him and we both enjoyed a loving relationship. I have learned that every moment, every word counts. I have learned that it is possible to not be able to breathe and still go on with life. I have learned humility, and understand that there are others that have experienced worse than I have and still continue on. I have learned to do what matters most…REALLY being in the moment, each and every moment with the people you care about. Slowing down and appreciating the moments I create every day, enjoying them while they happen. Feeling…whether it is pain or happiness, I'm letting myself feel it, breathe it, taste it, letting it fill me and give me release.

On God:

Since my son's death I have been obsessed with death and the afterlife…reading and learning are my comforts. I have read a multitude of books throughout my life, but never with such drive as I have been recently. I want answers, I want truth, and I need to know my child is okay, I need to know that there is more, that I will be with him again in some way. I believe there is a power greater than I, I feel it in me. How else would I be able to continue through this life if there was not some power holding me together, keeping me strong? That must be God. I don't believe that God picks and chooses who is to die, I believe that God is the energy that created us and put us here to experience all that this world has to offer, we have free will, the accidents that happen are the result of our choices whether we realize it or not we are choosing how our life will play out. I believe that God doesn't interfere with our lives but he is always with us, in us.

March 13, 2008

I find myself thinking in a fashion that this is reversible, that if I just come up with the perfect resolution it can be reversed. I wonder why other parents get to have 3 or more children and I only got two and now only have one. I have wondered why some parents are blessed with children when in my mind they certainly don't deserve them and the kids don't deserve the crappy life they have either. I know that life is not fair. I know that my son is dead, but my heart has not accepted it yet and may never. I see my son's life pass through my mind…the woman he would've been with, I picture him dressed in a tuxedo on his wedding day, and I feel the words we would say to each other-the love that would beam out of my pores. I see the pride in his eyes as he hands me his first born child. I also see Joshua as an only child with no one to turn to when I am gone, no one for his kids to call uncle. I pray that one of Josh's children is like Jonathon for both our sakes.

Being a parent is so hard. I want to be a great mom. I want to provide my kids with all the tools they will need to succeed in life. No matter what "success" means to them. I don't judge success by financial means; I see success as a state of mind. If in your true heart you feel that your life is fulfilling and you feel cherished and comfortable with yourself and who you are, then you are successful. You can have all the money in the world, but if you don't respect yourself and who you are, are you truly successful? I've felt success and I've felt failure and I will say that experiencing failure has made my success much more pleasurable.

March 16, 2008

I am a person who likes to ponder many thoughts…let things slide around in my head for a while. I enjoy thinking things through. I enjoy daydreaming, lazy thoughtless times, comfortable and content. I don't care to be rushed although I used to work best under pressure. I am a new person now. I feel like I am starting all over in getting to know myself. All I was content and happy with has been forever changed. My path is questionable. The challenges I am facing are overwhelming and I know somehow I will overcome them, but I wonder why I haven't believed in this strength before, it was there all along. As I think back, I see that I had it, and sometimes used it, but never realized it for what it was. I grew up seeing myself as a weak person incapable of taking care of myself, yet I spent a lot of time alone as a young teen taking care of my brother. As I look back I see the turning point in my life…it was becoming a mother. I was young and I definitely made mistakes, but I loved my baby with all my heart. I did the best I could with the tools I had available to me at the time. My self -esteem was low, but when I was taking care of my son I was as confident as a new mother is capable of being. Jonathon was my life, through him and later Josh; I grew courage and strength, but didn't see myself possessing it to the extent I have seen of late. I have had plenty of ups and downs in my life, which I have grown accustomed to and am very confident in the fact that I always spring back up, things always get better. I like that I know that. This is the longest and lowest I have ever been down, but again I have hope for the future I will struggle through this because I am meant to, but I will also come through with knowledge I didn't have before and hopefully a better sense of myself and the courage to follow my purpose.

I feel a presence in my soul; of words I do not have control your words they hold my body still while phantom breezes bring a chill, I feel your heartbeat with mine, the bittersweet, and the close divine. Stay near my child I'll hold you still, the day will come when I've had my fill and to your open arms I'll stride and feel the love and warmth inside

March 17, 2008

Everything I knew to be real is no more. My security and knowledge of the world have been destroyed. Losing my child in a car accident has ripped my world apart…I keep waiting for the other shoe to drop, what next? I actually have not been as worrisome as one would think would happen. I still cringe and do a mental check on where my family is every time I hear an ambulance siren, but I don't worry constantly when Josh is out driving or staying at a friend's house. I guess I have realized that I have no control over anyone's life; whatever is going to happen is going to happen. No advice or caution from me is going to keep my loved ones safe. I feel helpless, uncertain about anything and everything. Death is all around us and happens every day with no rhyme or reason and just because I lost one son doesn't mean the other can't be taken away also, there is no rule against it.

I always used to be waiting for things that were going to happen in my life, waiting to "live"…better job, more money, kid's to grow up, more time to relax, etc…but I now realize, this is my life, I was living my life. Life is what we do every day. John Lennon's quote is so true; "Life is what happens while we're busy making other plans." Right now my days are filled with motions, walking, talking, driving…I don't feel that I am connected to my body, I often wonder how I can actually focus on any task. It's hard to be out in the "world," I only want to interact with people of my choice. No conversations really interest me, I feel no joy at work as I did previously, I feel useless and in the way.

April 19, 2008

I cannot believe he is gone. I cannot imagine never seeing his face or hearing his voice again. I long for him daily; short, great pangs of longing. I cannot imagine all that will be missing in my life-all that I have lost. The passion for books and deep discussions we shared, his quick wit and intelligence, his dimpled smile. How at home he would walk around with a blanket wrapped around himself. I miss hearing him play his guitar, how he brought it to all family gatherings and would quietly play in the background. My love for him is so intense.

April 22, 2008

Life just keeps going…it doesn't wait for us to catch up, to catch our breath. All kinds of mediocre and not so mediocre issues come up every day and we are to function and deal with these situations even though our whole bodies are reeling from our loss. My judgment is lacking, my confidence has weakened. I have to re-think my whole being. Being Jonathon's mom was part of who I am, just like being Josh's mom is who I am. I know they are not the whole of whom and what I am, but right now it's difficult to see anything else…

I sit here on the roof…I feel the breeze on my face, hear the birds chirping, thinking of you.

April 28, 2008

I don't feel strong today; my confidence is fading away with my grief. I'm living in a nightmare. Nothing feels real. What is important? My body feels dead and ugly…the outside matching the in. There are no answers to my questions, there are only more questions. We learn by experience, by suffering- what am I learning? Where will it lead me? My resources lie within. I scramble and yearn to know how to use them, how to experience this and not lose myself. How do I serve my God, the universe, my family? Who am I? What do I believe? Who can I trust? What do I feel? What is real?

Random thought...

I see weakness in others and I deplore it...strange isn't it? I think it is because I deplore weakness in myself. I see my weaknesses reflected in other people...I work so hard to be the best person I can, and to make the most of who I am and it frustrates me when people refuse to acknowledge their weakness, refuse to see themselves how they really are. It's often because when we really look at ourselves, we are given a choice...accept what we see, for what it is, or do something to change it...and change is scary and hard.

Mother's Day 2008

Today I went to the site of Jonathon's accident...I put a poem I had written next to the cross there. I sat on the ground and I prayed for courage and strength to go on. I cried. For the first time I noticed the skid marks on the road...my heart hurts. As I was driving away I felt an urge to finish the drive that my son could not finish that foggy, Thursday morning in August last year. I was allowed to finish, he was not.

I miss my son; I pray that he didn't feel pain. I like to imagine that as he fell asleep at the wheel, he was dreaming and then woke up unto God, Light, Peace and Understanding. I only ever wanted him to be safe and happy and now he is both.

May 14, 2008

Tomorrow is my 40th birthday…What have I learned in those 40 years? So many things, some I realized as they were happening, others after I have looked back. Have I had a good life? Yes, I have. I'm stunned as I look back at that sentence…my son and my mom have died in the past 7 months and my world has been forever changed, yet I still believe my life has been good. Wow. In a way I have come so far, but yet have so much more yet to learn. My life has been good. I have known true love with a man. I have been given the gift of motherhood and I have been blessed with the ability to love and nurture my children. I have also been blessed with a fun, creative, passionate nature and I have used it well with them. Yes, my life has been good.

I often have a difficult time believing my life will be good or happy again. It's hard to imagine laughing or smiling and meaning it…In my heart I believe it could be. I know my mom and Jonathon would want me to be happy and not grieve for them too long. One day at a time, that's all I can ask for, that's all I can handle right now.

Looking back…

As I re-read my words, I see how many mountains and valley's my life has traveled. I notice many times where I have sunk so low and it was hard to imagine ever pulling myself out again. But as I read on I see where God has taken my heart and guided me up to a higher level and I feel strength and faith take hold of me once more. I think that is life in general whether you have experienced tragedy or not. Every life has its ups and downs and it's a matter of perspective, faith or whatever you need to call it that gives us the ability to pull ourselves up and out of our suffering. We all have that ability within us and it's a choice to use it or not. Personally, I choose hope and I trust that God has my back and that I am exactly where I need to be at any given moment.

May 16, 2008

It's so confusing how my emotions are all over the place…sometimes I feel as though I am on the verge of insanity, that I cannot bear one more moment of my life as it is. Other times I am exhilarated by life and the clarity at which I sometimes see things. No pattern…coming and going as it chooses. I feel as though I am living someone else's life…I'm confused and not sure how to respond. I feel suffocated by people, yet totally alone.

May 21, 2008

I'm not sure if we could ever really understand the true importance of life without having experienced the true loss of life. For me, having several people I love die so close together has really brought me to a new dimension of myself. I see myself and life differently on so many levels now. I have always been someone who is more in tune with myself than most, but it has recently become intensely more profound and real. I pray to God those feelings last and that I continue to have the courage and motivation to follow through to where they are leading me. Life continues to change and move forward, it is supposed to. How we handle life's ebb and flow tells a lot about who we allow ourselves to be.

Looking back...

Four months after my son died, I lost my mom to pancreatic cancer. My dad was coming to the end of his battle with Prostate cancer at this time also. I struggled with strong, conflicting emotions during this period in my life...grieving for my son, helping take care of my parents and watching them die, while also trying to be supportive for my youngest son and husband in their grief. There are no words to explain what I felt, if I even was even feeling at all.

I've said it many times since because I believe it to be true...God MUST be in me because there is NO other explanation for how I could have continued on without him during that truly difficult time in my life.

May 29, 2008

I'm watching my dad die. It breaks my heart and reaches into my depths to pull all my pain to the surface. I've lost so much in so little time, a complete system shock...I'm moving on automatic pilot. Our lives are so short, the last days so frightening.

I'm grateful that Jonathon didn't have to suffer a lengthy death. With my parents, I almost need the time to try to come to some kind of peace with our relationships. I really didn't need to say anything more to Jonathon. I trust that our feelings for each other were known and strong. I didn't need to say goodbye, but I would have liked to. I couldn't be there at the end for him or my mom, but I can be for my dad. I will do anything I can to help make his transition the best it can be and I pray that mom and Jonathon will be of comfort to us.

June 05, 2008

What I wish for my mom in heaven-is whatever it means to her, but this is how I see it for her...I see her in a beautiful garden that she has nurtured. I see a cute little house that blends into its natural surroundings. I see her digging in the dirt, humming to herself, feeling peaceful, joyful, at home. In the dusk, she is sitting in a comfy chair, on a cozy porch, drinking coffee and reading in the late light. She looks up to smile and wave as Jonathon is stopping by, guitar in hand. He says softly, "Hi, Honey Grandma", she gives him a hug and a kiss on the cheek, then he sits on the steps to strum his guitar quietly while she reads... my mom and Jonathon, completely at peace.

June 09, 2008

There is so much more to this life than I can imagine. I long for life to suck me into it, to strengthen my courage to live my dreams. Whether I succeed by the world's terms does not matter as long as I am completely experiencing my life, being present in my journey. I look forward to becoming a grandma, but hopefully not for a while yet. I want to surround myself with the people I love and that love me, but leaving plenty of room for individuality and time alone.

June 15, 2008

I don't want to feel this heavy sadness anymore. I carry its weight with me every day. I want to set it aside and live. The ones I have lost will always be with me and I know they wouldn't want anything but happiness for me. I want to remember that and set aside the rest. Letting go and letting God isn't as easy as it may sound. I struggle with control and it's difficult to just give that up, even to God. I feel responsible for my life, a responsibility to find my way through this, but I can't do it alone, I need God's guidance and strength to keep going. Sometimes I feel God so strong in me, and other days I feel so alone in my world.

June 25, 2008

How much more heartache can I possibly bear? Will there be a breaking point or am I strong enough to endure even more…? My mind is a mess and yet my body continues to go through the motions-moving forward. There is a power at work inside me; sometimes I feel it so strong, so powerful. But other times I feel like my body is dragging a confused and scared mind behind it, not giving it any choice but to move forward. It's like I'm in a dream state and all I want is to wake up and see that this isn't really my life.

July 13, 2008

My life is in turmoil, everything is getting crazy, and unreal…my strong, confident, ever supportive husband is not to be found. I feel like he is lost to me, and I don't know how to bring him back or if I even want to try. I don't know what he wants or expects from me now. I don't know if I can be the person he thinks he is looking for. I feel a big turning point coming, which way will I choose, what will bring me closer to my purpose? Only God knows.

I miss Jonathon with all my being, it still doesn't seem real. This is my life…

August 2008

My relationship of 22 years with my husband has come to a sad ending. The statistics say this happens often in cases with the death of a child. Our relationship was strong and healthy and yet in this time of great sorrow, we have not been able to provide each other with the support we needed. It's almost as if we can't bear to see the pain in each other's eyes and hearts. We are no longer the people we were before our son died. As every aspect of our lives was changing we somehow allowed another person to come between us and move us even further apart. Another jolt to my senses...how much more must I endure? I am strong in faith and hope; I will prevail...somehow, someway...

September 01, 2008

So many thoughts, never enough words to express the passionate, strong power that resides in me. I have wonderful thoughts, ideas – my pen cannot keep up. I crave to share these thoughts with others. I believe I have the gift of insight, a great attitude about life in general. I have so much to offer, so much to share. I want to help others get through the tough times in life and not just get through them, but learn from them, grow from them. We can either allow life to drag us down, or stay strong and know that "this too shall pass." I also believe that it is possible to end up in a better state of mind because of the trials of life. There can be much sadness and pain, but there is also much beauty and love to behold.

September 12, 2008

I'm feeling weak and defeated today...I'm so tired of thinking, trying to be strong and calm. I want to throw things, yell, scream, punch, slap, kick and pulverize, then lay my head down on my mom's lap and cry like a baby...but none of those things will happen, I am a calm person and my mom is no longer on this earth. I don't know how to make myself take the actions I know I must. I'm tired, scared and feeling very alone.

October 03, 2008

I had a profound moment today…I've had a couple really crappy weeks and yet another situation to figure out…Josh needs me to be strong and supportive of him in his life and I feel so helpless. He's my baby; I want him to be happy, to laugh, have fun and to get through all this hurt. The realization that he is struggling more than I thought is just too much to handle right now…I want to just curl up on the floor, go to sleep and escape reality and I did just do that. But I lay there just a few minutes before it came to me that I could either continue to lay there feeling sorry for myself which would do no one any good or I could get off my butt, pull myself together and be an example for Josh. I realize in these brief moments that I can and will handle what I need to and with my example and guidance so will Josh. God is with us, even when it doesn't feel like it.

October 18, 2008

Life just keeps right on moving along, whether we are ready or not. Josh and I have suffered much pain in the past two years; it would be great if we could get some breathing room for a little bit. Just to have a break to deal with what we have already been given, but it seems to just keep on coming.

In a way I am grateful for the things I have learned in life recently. I am stronger and more capable of taking care of myself than I thought. I am more confident and not as afraid to take risks to experience life more fully. I am totally confident in the fact that I am a good mom and my children have always loved me very much. Life is too short to sit around feeling sorry for myself and it doesn't do any good anyway. Only I am responsible for my own happiness. Sometimes, I get this overpowering desire to "Live," I feel overwhelmed with this burning feeling to really experience each moment...hearing, seeing, smelling and feeling it, right here, right now. Good, bad or other, to just be in it...

October 20, 2008

I don't know anything about myself anymore; nothing seems sure for too long, I feel confident and strong in so many conflicting ways. I don't know what reality is. Are the people around me aware of my confusion and uncertainty? Does it show on my face, in my actions? Do I make sense when I speak? Or am I really being this strong force that I feel most of the time?

October 26, 2008

Sorrow and grief, bear down on my heart
but I refuse to give in, I will not fall apart
The burdens I carry are mine alone to bear
But the hope that I feel, I will lovingly share
For God has given me a chance, to stand tall and be strong
He's shown me great courage, when all seems to go wrong
I'm blessed with a gift, to see hope in all things
I'm ready and willing, to take all that life brings
I will make the most of each moment, in all that I do
Live life to its fullest, and to myself be true.

November 03, 2008

I miss Jonathon so much today…sitting here at the park; I remember all the time we spent here when the kids were younger. I am so heartbroken by my loss…we understood each other, our uniqueness, our love of words and books, our passion for what we believed in. I have that with no one else. I have lost a friend as well as a child. I hurt for the unfairness of it all, the senseless loss, my aching to hear his voice, to see his face, to just be near him. I feel alone in the sense that he was the only one who really "got" me. He understood my craziness, my quirks, just as I understood his. My world feels empty without him in it. My hope for future discussions as he matured, books we would have talked about, ideas we would have shared…shattered. I feel cheated and betrayed by God in a sense. I am a good mom; I didn't deserve to lose a child. I am scared that I won't be able to help Josh come through this all okay. What if I fail him? What will our lives be like without Jonathon? Who will Josh have when Jon and I are no longer on this earth, now that his only sibling is gone? Who will he talk to about his childhood, who will he remember with?

November 08, 2008

To Jonathon:

I remember the last time I saw you alive...at the bottom of the stairs, early in the morning. You had just finished work and stopped over for a bowl of cereal and a bottle of body wash...it was close to payday and you were out. I recall waking up and coming down the stairs and saying good morning and wishing you a good day. I remember speaking to you on the phone the day before you died. Hearing you tell me you loved me and saying it back. The very next morning life as I knew it was over.

Sometimes I feel like I have neglected you in my grieving...I've had so many sad things happen in such a short time, that I haven't only thought of you. I know that thought is unreasonable, but it's still there. I know, you and Honey Grandma don't want me to be sad and I know that you both are very proud of the way I am handling myself. I thank you Jonathon for the courage you showed in being true to yourself, no matter what. Even though sometimes it was frustrating to watch, I was still proud of you for it and I totally get it now. I am using your example and being true to the person I know that I am. I miss you so much!

November 09, 2008

Is it really possible that this strength, hope and optimism are real? It feels real. A friend tells me that it's just a front, that I'm just covering up my feelings…So being the deep thinker that I am; I took a look at that. What I have concluded is that it feels real to me and what is wrong with feeling positive and grateful in the face of tragedy? I have my down times; days when it feels like I can't breathe and I just don't want to deal with the world. But I have many outlets for my grief, writing and reading being the top two and I do have people that support me. I am very proud of myself for the enlightenment I am allowing into my life. I am being true to who I am.

November 12, 2008

Confusion-nothing seems real. Do I really consciously know what I am doing? Sometimes I wonder. I go to work every day, perform the tasks, things get done. I come home and do nothing. I've misplaced my motivation. I think too much, I always have, I feel I'm sinking back into my solitude- I DON'T WANT TO DO THAT! It's so hard to come out of it on my own sometimes, but I will, I have to, I must rely on myself. I'm the only one I can count on; with God as my strength I will fight to stay afloat. Sometimes I am scared to death, but I have faith that I will figure it out and work through it.

November 26, 2008   Thanksgiving day

Its 9 am, I'm sitting outside and it's a beautiful morning. Today is a day of giving thanks and I am thinking about the many things I have to be thankful for. I am thankful for each new day I am given to be with the people I care about. I am thankful for my children, the 20 years that I had with Jonathon and every moment that I get to spend with Josh. I am thankful for the people that have been supportive of me through these tough times. I am blessed in many ways.

Later same day...

I am a strong, confident, self-reliant woman. I am capable of taking care of my own needs. I will concentrate on being in service to God, I will be the best me I can be. I know that only I am responsible for my own happiness. I will surround myself with positive influence. I will be confident in my choices. I will take the actions that stand for who I am and where I am going.

December 08, 2008

An "Aha" moment…

In August of 2007 my son died, in November of same year my mom died from Pancreatic cancer, in June 2008 my dad died from Prostate cancer, and in July the same year my husband left me. My life has been a crazy, surreal, chaotic train wreck. The people in my life that I counted on have either died, left me or are just too uncomfortable with my situation to be of any support.

The day it hit me, I was sitting in my room, randomly writing in my journal when I had a feeling that is hard to describe…I realized that we really are all alone in the world. God is in us and that is all we can really count on. I believe that as long as I live in good faith, God will provide me with the support and strength that I need. Maybe we really aren't given more than we can handle.

December 11, 2008

I sit on the roof in the cool night air, I breathe in the crispness…I feel you sitting next to me as you used to. When I look at the stars I recall the vastness of your mind, and how you and grandpa loved looking into the night sky. I miss our debates, so much that it physically hurts. I miss your blue eyes and dimples, your voice and your smart-ass grin. I still can't believe you are gone, that I will never feel you again. I love you so much, why did you have to leave us so soon?

December 14, 2008

My life feels so out of control- I forget that I never really was in control. It has always been in God's hands. I pray that God's strength continues to carry me and Josh through these tough times. I have hope for better days...I can't wait for spring and the feeling of renewal- a fresh start.

December 18, 2008

My son has died...The reality of it hits me hard

Takes my breath away...I face it every day

In every area of my life...The cruel harshness of it

The irrevocable truth...My mind is a mess

Confusion rules...Struggling to stay afloat

To think rational thoughts...To breathe

Nothing makes sense for very long...

So many feelings...Crashing into each other

So tired of being so tired

Waiting and working towards being happy

A new sense of the word...

Whatever it means now

January 09, 2009

Why I choose to be positive...

My life has so far given me many wonderful moments and experiences- I have given birth to two healthy children. I have nurtured and loved them. Most of the best experiences in my life have been with my boys. That is my greatest blessing, one I will be forever grateful for. I have loved and been loved deeply, I have had many wonderful, precious and thrilling moments in my marriage. I have been surrounded with animals and have been blessed with their loyal admiration. I have lived in the house of my dreams and have experienced many, many happy moments with my family there. I truly have been blessed.

At this point in my life, I have lost one of my children, my marriage, my best friend and my home. I choose to be positive because I know I can't change any of the things that have happened, they are done. I choose to be positive because I still have a living son that I love with all my heart, who will have children that I can't wait to meet and love. I choose to be positive because I believe God has a purpose for me and he is giving me the strength to fulfill it. I choose to be positive because I refuse to be swallowed up in pain and anger. I choose to be positive because I know I have many more moments of joy and happiness in front of me and every single day I have something to be grateful for.

January 18, 2009

Are you playing guitar in heaven
In the early evening light,
Or sitting quietly in the silence,
Reading to your hearts delight
Is debating every topic, still your favorite thing to do
And are you busy gaining knowledge…
From the great minds in heaven with you?

February 09, 2009

What do I look like to you
Can you see what is inside, all the pain that I hide
Can you see my fatigue or my longing and need
Can you see my sadness when you look in my eye
Do I look hideous behind my disguise

Late 2009

As I re-read these pages from my journals, I struggle not to feel the pull of these words, these moments and emotions. I'm careful not to linger in the past too long but move forward, always forward. Looking at these pages from my life allows me to see how far I have come, how much I have grown. The pain is not gone, only different, always there but somehow a little more bearable. There are more and more moments where I feel good, somewhat excited and yes, even optimistic. I believe more good things will come... I still have a long way to go in my healing, and maybe it never ends but I have Hope...

Final note:

As with you dear reader, my story does not end here. My son's tragic death will be part of my life forever. There will be a void in my heart for all of my days. But if I have brought anything to you with my words, I pray that it has been a feeling of Hope and the knowledge that we all have a purpose. Our children that have died are somehow serving their purpose for God. It is not for us to determine the when, where, how or why...we can't know God's plan. It is for us though, to continue with our lives, the very best we can and grow from our experiences so we may fulfill our purpose.

God Bless.

Julie Bergstrom

THE END

Made in the USA
Monee, IL
05 July 2023

38714220R00046